KASHMIR IS HEAVEN ENOUGH

poems

FARHANA QAZI

Newport
PUBLISHING

ALSO BY FARHANA QAZI

Secrets of the Kashmir Valley

Untold Truths of the Kashmir Valley

Invisible Martyrs

Kashmir Is Heaven Enough
Farhana Qazi

Copyright 2024 by Farhana Qazi
Cover Design by Maryam Ali
Book design and type formatting by Hamza Azeem

Library of Congress Cataloging-in-Publication Data

Qazi, Farhana, 2024
Kashmir Is Heaven Enough

Printed in the United States of America

ISBN 978-0-9994102-4-0 pbk

www.farhanaqazi.com

To the people of Kashmir

Agar firdaus bar ru-ye zamin ast
Hamin ast-o-hamin ast-hamin ast

If there is Paradise on earth,
it is this, it is this, it is this.

— Sufi poet Hazrat Amin Khusrau

Table of Contents

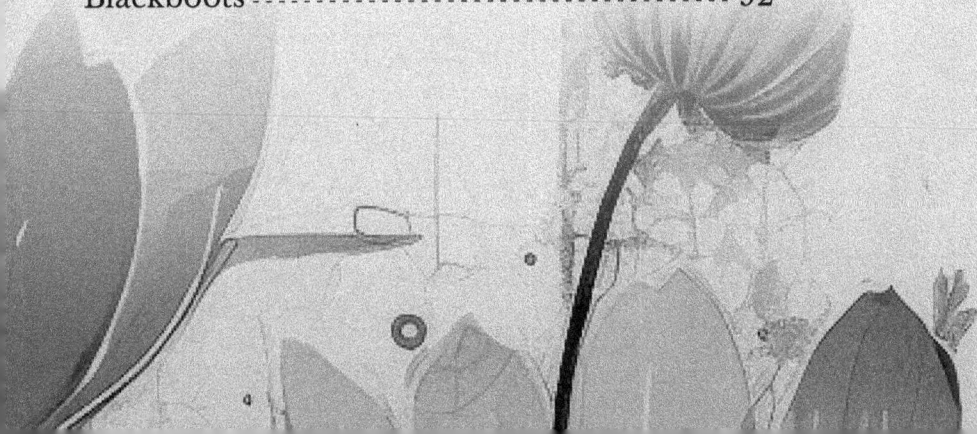

Note

Travels to Kashmir are an unforgettable experience. In this collection of verse, tragedy meets beauty, and joy greets oppression as the morning sun rises and night sinks into the earth. I entered a world of paralyzing beauty, swooping walls of ice in winter and the most dramatic landscape of dense forest, magical gardens, and clear lakes in the summer. A place where everything is perfectly still while also seemingly alive as if breathing, blossoming, with kingfisher birds swooping by cities under siege.

Kashmir is a Wonderland of pristine lakes, ice-blue mountains, and friendly locals. It isn't easy to reach the world's highest conflict zone, but the rewards are bountiful. The valley of green unfolds with a rich history of artisans, a traditional culture of storytelling, and love ingrained in everything they do. This is a place where anyone can feel connected to family and culture; everyone is warmly hospitable. No one is unsafe with the locals.

Coined Paradise on earth, Kashmir comes alive with vibrant colors and characters—a version of paradise compared to the alps of Switzerland and Asia's Shangri-La. Here, life can be both spectacular and suffocating.

In the historic valley, trauma is felt everywhere. Locals cope with everyday stress by holding onto compassion, hope, and faith. They share stories of the dead and sing songs for the present. Most Kashmiris join peaceful protest movements; a few fight with weapons and rage.

From my travels, I remember nights, held under the canopy of stars, feeling breathless by the immense beauty of the quarter moon and the valley, sleeping and silent. I remember mornings of birdsong and colors of a mango sun rising in this otherworldly paradise with picture-perfect greens and panoramic views of ancient castles creating a play of light and shadow inside each home.

Wherever I went, I was protected by the locals and discovered a love that held people together, strong and steady. In every village and city, there was an unpunctured sense of ease and effortlessness in daily interactions, conversations of cherished times and gratitude for staying alive. Locals comforted me, and despite the horrors of conflict, I had the luxury of safety and a way back home to America.

Human stories are the heart of resistance. This book honors the beauty of the valley and the people inside it. These verses are a tribute to those who disappeared or died unjustly. And to those who are alive, present and patient for a future of freedom and joy. I will never forget you, Kashmir.

Feb. 12, 2024

Farhana Qazi

In This Place

In the valley of Kashmir,
I am lost and found.
Mountains are swept
by veils of rain and snow.

In the valley of death,
everyone protested, shouted.
Cries of freedom rise
into hot, summer air.

In the valley of truth,
I am free and caged.
Cities and villages are
the heartbeat of resistance.

In the valley of green,
everyone is absorbed, anxious.
Encounters remind us
that nothing is normal here.

Wonderland

So much has changed in Paradise, where curving walls of ice are deflected by the sun and vivid shades of cobalt and aquamarine, everything still and silent, breathing and alive even as death is near. The woman I loved most passed away with grief; a teenage boy with golden-brown hair shot on the cricket field; a father jailed for writing books; and human rights activists disappeared or dead.

The conflict is oppressive.

Only a microscopic fraction of the world live here. The valley of green-blue is divided between India, Pakistan and the Aksai Chin region of China—a people among clumps of snow and bitingly cold temperatures are plunged into darkness, their lives passing like slow-motion pictures while militaries engage in tit-for-tat border clashes like bullies in the highest battlefield and kill without reason or permission.

Kashmir is an open wound.

The war has a feeling of suffocation, an expectancy and anxiety, reflected in study circles, writing workshops, and online forums, exposing decades of injustice by men in black boots trudging up mountains and hills of dense forest or wading across rivers, brown with rain. Even in their grief, locals have permission to build something beautiful. Something true. They have a right to speak up.

Wonderland is marked by resistance.

In Darkness

A quiet dots the hillside, people in pinto-box homes over
blue-green lakes and forests, fragile and deep.
By nightfall, the women turn, hands across children's
tiny backs, whispering a sea of syllables, songs of old
used in ancient times for uninterrupted sleep.

Kashmir is enigmatic and frightening.

As night thickens, the sky opens to predators, a shadow army
stomps on human earth, cool water, and fragrant flowers
along the road. They trudge over cliffs covered in vegetation,
climbing over rocks where the
first people lived, and stop at the village, pitch-dark.

Kashmir is ambiguous and unexpected.

When daylight breaks, local men cut through tall grass and
trees, followed by small feet. Boys survive by learning their
fathers' ways, and women kneel to prayer for their safety
begging the Beloved to keep men in black boots with old
anger away.

Kashmir is blindsiding and brutal.

As time passes, kingfishers glide and gyre over villages and cities festering in frustration, a valley of people grieving, worrying, and condemning the occupation that strangles human consciousness and leaves behind worst-case scenarios of trauma. By day or night, life and death happen without notice.

Kashmir is erratic and sudden.

Locals wait for the light to break and blue-white ice to give way to spring. They wait for kind, gentle surprises, a morning sun high and hot to filter its light through the forest and onto the horizon of dark clouds hanging like low fruit over the mountain.

Kashmir is (almost) heaven enough.

The Jhellum River

My voice fades almost to silence
in the vast land called Kashmir,
where names of mountains
sound like tribes, and people are forever
trapped between ice, blue-green fields
of summer and tulip gardens
tourists come to see, with one eye open,
blind to the tragedies that unfold
under a heroic blue sky in a place
where women hold pictures of their dead,
under the shade of a towering chinar
and leaves turn a burnt orange in fall.

In mornings laced with birdsong,
I fill notes with verbs and broken nouns,
unable to describe a corrugated house
on top of hills in a heartland
with castles named after fairies
and monuments for leaders, great
and then gone; standing on top of the cliff.
I see streams, peat-brown, flowing into
the mighty Jhelum—water and wind racing
against time in a valley of motion.

Snow

On the map are hills in vertical zigzags,
mountains in an unbroken swell
and sketches of trees racked by the wind.
Nights too cold for sleep is a quiet
renaissance, the aloneness a gift for lovers
lying in the dark. Here, the drum of critters
in a far-off secluded hill is a vestigial
blessing, unexpected in a valley of miracles.
Only sheep climb through deepening snow.

Forgotten

In semi-darkness, the path ascends,
the moon in serrated shadows.
We walk together over heavy hills
through village lights along the road.

We approach the green lamp,
the entrance to the mammoth house
filled with a family's belongings:
an island of toys, a picture of a boy
in green eyes, his toothbrush and cups
black with cardamon, unwashed.

It was here.

Things, like icons, spread across
dusty shelves in a room weathered
with pain. The neighbors leave them
alone, afraid to bring back memories
of children, happy and free.

They are gone.

We move beyond eastern peaks separated
by white-green trunks of fallen trees and
hear the sound of the river thundering
across fallen homes where women
once prayed to saints for mercy.

They cry for missing boys.

Paradise on Earth

Silence fills the night air, flirting
with the sheen of a mother-of-pearl moon,
its light still on placid waters that will disappear
by morning when an incandescent orange
rises over Kashmir.

It is here.

This is a valley of endless colors and shapes,
untraceable by artists with paintings of scenes
from memory or wanting lovers with stories of old,
using words to visualize in color,
their description of the land as
wide, empty country.

It is here.

The savage force of storms and the torrent
of floodwater that damages houseboats
are softened by the rhythmic beat
of small animals, their noises loud
and raw under the stars.

It is here.

The calm of morning white, the red strands of
evening sun, and blue-green fields is silent
harmony reflected through the eyes of trees
on dark, cold nights—images of a valley,
magical and free in spirit.

Kashmir is Paradise on earth.

The Yellows

In summer, the yellows thread
through the forest in soft lemon light.

The centuries-old landscape is untouched
by darkness and a shadow army.

A mosaic of colors spiral across the sky
as the heartbeat of a cold sun dances.

Kashmir is Heaven enough.

Mugli

He leads the way,
a man of honey-beige eyes
and hands, small and hard.
We cross an alley of homes,
candles flickering inside.
The wind's breath is heavy
in curfewed nights.
He whispers, leaning in.
Be careful, look ahead,
as we head down a labyrinth
looking for 'the lonely mother.'
She opens the door, kind and
frail from years of searching
for a ghost that was once her
beloved son—she is a witness
to time and death.
In unshakeable breath,
she offers praise and love:
you are too beautiful for the moon.
We hold each other tightly
in a familiar embrace.
We leave with heavy hearts;
her words linger long after that
silent night of icicles and cold wind.
Years later, the image of her face
glows like a pale egg, and I hear
her voice, screaming for love.
Mugli is unforgotten.

Fallen

Their heads bob like sparrows. Women in white mourn the
passing of a great leader, their first revolutionary killed in blue-
green cold on the stones of brown-gray cliffs in a conquered city
where soldiers outnumber locals.

A wounded voice calls the army.

You killed another innocent.

Women hunch over bodies wrapped in white, motionless and
unable to speak their truth. Mothers hold onto prayer beads
and read from holy books until the dead are moved in ice
sheets to the deep ground.

A mother sighs to the Sky.

He was only a boy.

Child's Play

a girl with luminous eyes
searches for play in bare feet

let's go!

she calls to boys to join her
in high laughter and songs of old

let's play!

they chase each other to the beat
of black boots and army trucks

let's run!

they escape into the black forest,
and pray to the rain-filled sky

The Storm

Everything changes. At first, it comes in the shape of a pond until the water flows out of the soil, growing wider and deeper. Water rises and locals climb to roof tops.

The ground is swelling. Icy water penetrates deeper into their bones, and the river is relentless; bridges and mountain peaks fall with a vengeance, and animals float.

The Beloved is angry. The valley of green may soon disappear, leaving a ghostly memory of trees over rock as the river rushes past limbs who cannot swim.

The sun is barely visible. After the storm, they find a safe space from puddles of cotton grass and hold each other, unable to speak of what they have lost in feather gray soil.

Kashmir is alive.

Danger

they move in and out of porous borders,
clinging to weapons and each other;
men in camouflaged faces and khakis
glide across mountain peaks, chased by
an army on the hunt.

men in uniform are wounded by war,
and soldiers dream of normalcy in chaos:
masala-rich food, warm conversations
and sweet chai as their children play
without gunfire or shelling.

we are the lucky ones; we can sleep again,
take afternoon walks over green-black
water grass, the wind combing tall grass,
and watch the sunrise catch a golden
glow over a dark forest.

everything changes in war

by night, young men in cold mountain
slide down to their village with stories
of survival and death; they never forget,
their kangaroo eyes scan the cliffs for danger,
and feel anger for what they have lost.

a known enemy hides with weapons in hills,
as boys crawl down silver-gray mountain
breathless and tired feet; children pass by
fields of saffron and frozen lakes, searching
for the next hiding spot.

the lucky few celebrate life for a moment
and wait for new seasons to melt rectangular
ice with warm light; they pray they will live
to fall in love and play with future children,
letting go of all the terrible things.

nothing is normal in war

Half Light,
Half Shadow

Small, white blossoms dot the ground,
trembling in the wind as women dance in open
air for a new bride or child born into a family
to forget the tragedies of the past year.

No one whispers the names of the dead,
as song and dance linger into the night,
women clapping, their shadows circling
the wall like fairies in ancient stories.

They celebrate and forget their men over
jagged rock, half-frozen and stained by pain,
their bitter hearts ready for vengeance
and a promise to take back their land.

War makes death inevitable; their hearts fill
with new vows to defeat the angel of death
and men grab their guns to fight another day.

In half light, half shadow, everyone breaks.

Bravura

men in black boots slump in army trucks
trudging along a deep green forest, and not
a trace of bravura in the whites of their eyes

in uniform, they stroll by Dal Lake, smoking
staring, smiling at women, sensing danger
until heavy ran flattens water lilies

men of might run from hard rain

for a moment, they pretend to be invisible,
as crackling sounds of shelling like distant
cannon spreads fear through the valley

the youth will not give up until they fall

the valley surrenders to the dead;
boys become tangled in yellow grass,
and women wail by the fire of the *kangari*

Unspoken

She opens her notebook and writes what she knows: a people oppressed by fanatic rule and freedom songs inspired by America's civil rights leaders who demanded to be free.

Here, the valley is torn by forest guerrillas and the army. She scribbles words only she can recognize, letters of tragedy mute her laughter and childlike joy. She reads to herself: my uncle died in an encounter and brother hit by pellet guns.

Here, the valley mourns children who have not yet lived.

She is afraid to share her notebook, filled with stories of pain, boorish and cruel. She belongs to a generation that counts the dead and wishes for her mother's arms to heal the hurt.

Here, the valley is filled with secrets and sorrow.

Hope and Light

we imagined summers passing in a slow, damp embrace,
inventing tales of tender, gentle love in a world that
nurtures human life and fills hearts with
compassion and courage

this place is haunted and real, a magical mystery,
barely alive with peonies in winter and
tulips in spring, a brief reminder
that beauty can survive
great tragedy

we put aside stories of suffering and acute pain,
so that we can experience strange love,
the kind that closes hurt and harm
and brings back passion
in young hearts

we are not alone in what we feel or know,
even if we keep secrets for a lifetime;
there will always be moments
of twilight in early spring
and light rain

one day, this will pass; the oppression will subside
as gray-white ice melts over mountains
when the air is warm, dry, and you
hold me closer, filled with
hope and light

Unmarked Graves

we have a right to choose an intentional life because we are capable and resilient; we are a brave people deserving circles of joy and play over wet ground under an orange sun

we are fearless and filled with limitless potential to change the world, if we are given a chance to rise above pain and create new stories filled with hope and happiness

our shared vulnerability is invisible to everyone outside the valley; we scream for attention so others can feel the sorrow of generations as we weep for unmarked graves

we are not supposed to live this way, and our humanness chooses joy, bliss and peace; for centuries, we have mourned over ashes and dust, corpses with names we know

we are strong, no matter how dark it is, and how long we may have to cry, scream, and fight for small things and big lives; our experiences of death is how you will remember us

Longing for You

On days when the sun is barely visible, she retreats into her father's workshop to record the first words of her lover. Like other girls, she hopes for a perfect love.

I will not forget you. I will love you still.

He has been gone for a long time, somewhere in Central Jail. Some say he's forever lost between despair and quietude, unknowing when he might be released.

I am not the same person. I barely exist.

In the darkest nights, she frames her own death in words she cannot say out loud. She is dying while living, and this ugly truth explains everything.

I don't know how long I can wait. I cannot survive this.

Untold Truth

Here, there is more tragedy than most see in a lifetime: villages besieged by the madness of conflict and a desperate cry for freedom permeates the air. *We are barely living.*

Love is Enough

Trust the Beloved and you will find love in a place held captive by soldiers scared of reprisals. You say you are tired of running through alleyways and over green hills to escape captivity. I say we can meet in the middle of conflict and take back our hearts. At least we can find love.

Can we forget that we exist among rebel songs, missing men, and firing in the fields? Can we pretend we live outside of war and let go of enduring loneliness? Can we find love in the light of stars and a deep blue moon? Is love enough to survive the impurities of conflict?

Trust in love, even if we become wandering exiles and will never touch the valley of gold, a sacred land that holds hearts and homes in times of crisis. Have faith in me and give this a chance; believe that our desire is the miracle.

Love can be our Paradise on earth.

The Next Life

They know they are dying in the forever war.

No politician, protestor, or pacifist can offer calm from the secrets that burn their hearts on moonless nights when the darkness enfolds the valley and disrupts ordinary routines.

Everything is extraordinary here: large crowds, water lilies blossoming on Dal Lake, the smell of your skin after morning rain, and that suffering (the inescapable kind) will pass.

After seventy plus years of fear, false promises, and facts unchecked. No one bends to violence without a reason; the boys are unafraid to lose what they do not own and join groups to feel.

They believe land is worth fighting for.

Boys pretend to be significant, portentous, powerful. With resistance songs, and bands of warm light, the youth come alive, their love for the next life stronger than living among the dead.

Most take to the streets in protest, calling for an end to occupation, and exist somewhere between fear and fury. If theydie, martyrs will sleep in gardens of bliss and live on.

In the heavens, the secrets of dying men and women are told in gold-green; they will experience love without anxiety or agitation. Without pain or panic. Only the right to euphoria.

The gates of Jannah is open to the believers.

Generations of innocent children and adults stained by conflict belong here, alongside angels of free will and messengers with wings. They deserve a lifetime of comfort denied on earth.

In the next life, traumas felt for the trillionth time and the smell of corpses in deep ground is erased. Here, they will meet family lost in war and can choose stillness or laughter for eternity.

Martyrs know the demons that make living impossible; they embrace death and walk into dark forests to change the life they never had. The next life is their only destination.

Paradise is worth dying for.

Beauty

In summer, local boys swim in the lake with the sun on their backs; children run up and down the stairs to the entrance of the Mughal garden lined with peonies and pink roses.

In autumn, red amaranth blossoms perfume the inner walls of the palace and pigeons flock to the fountain under a cloudless blue sky as locals walk by a nest of tree leaves.

In winter, royal blue snowflakes fall like jewels and a slow frost sends tourists inside; few reporters lag behind to tell their version of a complicated story of conflict.

Hotels along Boulevard Road lie empty in winter, and swimming pools are covered in ice sheets; in empty castles, sunflowers lean towards the fierce wind.

As spring arrives, a shikara decorated in silk gold curtains floats alongside houseboats stranded like vessels, and the rain fills the air with the smell of wood.

Quietude

At sunset, the city lights of Srinagar dim along the main road; robes of darkness conceal everything: the ox lying in the middle of the street, huts perched on mountaintops, and a fortress on top of a stony hill built by the third Mughal Emperor Akbar.

In quiet solitude, we are the happiest we have been in a long time. No gunfire. No sirens. No running. Only the sound of wind's breath and a lover's slow, humid embrace. We lie in the snow and watch a distant army hide in barracks.

From the castle, we spot a house and a ribbon of river that winds against the road as men in green-black stand on guard. We see a valley burst with abundant grace and remain still as stars blend into the hazy night sky.

In our silence, we are wild and compassionate, drenched in bucolic beauty: sheep graze among walnut trees and lush hills line the riverbanks even as soldiers pass them by. Together, our only fear is wasting time.

Paradise Bound

The sun keeps falling into the river, and they keep moving across the valley with fortitude and fierce rage. In this quiet cinematic moment, we are waiting for something to happen. Here, clashes happen frequently, and we are forced into the grassy field until the shelling stops.

The armed struggle survives the blizzard, and soldiers move steadily, scanning headlights at passing cars and late-night drivers. Armored tanks saturate our city: Paradise is a war zone and a tourist haven, a place where beauty meets tragedy.

No one can escape the grief.

We survive this to share stories and different versions of the truth, so anyone on the outside can make sense of shadows and silence, hearts thick with trapped rhythms, and funerals in afternoon light. We honor the seen and unseen, and long for something more than a lover's breath.

If there is Paradise on earth, it is here

In the valley that holds the worst news, this is a place where light is a threat, and speaking up against misery in the brink of daylight ignites violence. If Paradise is here, then there are wings everywhere, ready to rise above the earth and into the sky.

If Paradise lies in the folds of Kashmir, then nothing is lost and everything is certain. Hopes are tangled in shadow and secrets grow as though penned in a cage. Even so, no person of faith can be haunted by strange shapes forever.

Heaven is closer than the sound of light.

Landscape of Ruination

War touches everything. Love and death pass as fragments of everyday life. One person lives to witness random acts of violence, experience a cycle of abuse that empowers young men to move to the mountains with a chronicle of Kashmir's personal tragedies. These are the boys fighting to take back their dreams.

the color of a yellowing corpse is buried by thousands

When cold sculpts the landscape, vertical crystals grow along knife-edged peaks of known mountains, and boys ready for battle sleep along loose rock and gravel splintered by ice. They prepare to attack in spring and hope to live to see the army's downfall.

shadows of death are more terrifying than blurred light

They cling wildly to fantasies of freedom and forget decades of brutality against rebels before them, jailed for wanting more. The youth call for azadi in open air until they are taken away by the police and beaten by rods. Their cries inspire women to come out of their homes and protest the insanity of conflict.

the demand for justice is disrupted by the firing squad

The light of a false dawn from a silver sky alerts the youth that it's time to leave. They trudge along the seams of the valley in silence, convinced that land will be theirs when the army withdraws. If only the land of ruination could return to its original glory of forests, thick and green.

the valley begs for mercy and an end to violence

Belonging

She felt at home in a valley where the sun drifted inexorably toward the horizon. This was not just another day or nightfall approaching until light breaks along the lake. The village asked her to come back to celebrate love together. She wanted to vanish, to be fictitious and unfound by the people who needed her most. Her love had to be a guarded secret or she risked endangering a man once jailed for wishing freedom.

In a place far from Kashmir, she celebrated her love, alone and with simplicity, in honor of the timeless ritual. At night, she danced in spirals of joy and then slipped outside to see a billion stars pulse overhead. But no matter how hard she tried, she could not forget her ancestral home. Her love for Kashmir existed in amber light, and while she was at least free, everyone she loved lived with the burden of conflict.

FARHANA QAZI

The Pilgrims Land

From afar, they came for forest bathing and snow-capped
shrines and wanted to feel its famed power in this sacred land.
Many dreamt of walking the landscape, which was unforgiving
to anyone who raced across the dome of sky without caution.
Soon, the tenuous grassland and silver fir gave way to pilgrims
in a place called Yusmarg where Jesus is believed to have once
lived.

True to its name, Yus is for Jesus and marg means meadow;
the valley opened its heart to spiritual seekers and guides
at the same time every season. Every believer visited the
valley in search of eternal peace inside temples and mosques;
shrines and saints; and the mirrors of placid lakes.

Elsewhere, kingfishers flew in circles as pilgrims turned to faith
for comfort and looked inside vertical books, thousands of pages
long, inscribed with the names of holy men. When pilgrims
arrived, they found absolute silence and stared at the movements
of cloud silhouettes, scudding across the floor of the valley in
cumulus shapes.

When they looked up, they became ambiguous to the valley's pain, big and small. They arrived in Kashmir for personal gain, pretending the monsters did not exist, and forgot that savages treaded through leafless trees with a vengeance; victims of conflict once again burdened with taking care of outsiders who did not care to understand. If the pilgrims stayed, would they feel responsible for the future of Kashmir?

When the sacred rituals ended, pilgrims packed and paraded across the hills in patterned footsteps, chanting or whispering to the Beloved and indulged in spiritual graces until the next dusk. They roamed the valley like sheep, free and drifting, unbothered by death anniversaries and martyrs' graves; theirs was a casual hike into the trees with rhymed words.

Every year, the devout returned in saintlike robes, selfpossessed by hallowed voices on summer nights. The army opened the path for the pilgrims, so they were unharmed and practiced tradition, untroubled, and guided by breath and the sounds of the forest until they reached Paradise. When the rituals ended, the pilgrims retreated while the rest of the valley surrendered to rapturous sorrow

Where We Belong

We wake up each morning, ready to meet love and ask for more patience and peace. We beg for air with the fragrance of flowers, musky and deep. We are attached to the beauty and ugliness of the valley: the hazy rings of light on mountain tops, the unbreakable strength of women, and the barbaric acts of men.

This is our home. We survive days, weeks and months of silence, curfew, blackouts, and bullying by the army. We are a forgotten people, and families live with physical harm and psychological trauma. We cling wildly to fantasies of freedom even as some run away in blistering speed.

We experience life and death on the same day and fall hopelessly in love with gardens of torrential beauty and mountain shadow. The primal emotions of pleasure, anger, and despair is part of our history. This is our normal: a paranoia of living in a place drenched in grief while we wait for a safer tomorrow.

This is where we belong. In-between loss, love, faith, and trauma. We escape to empty castles, where we linger for love, and dream of a time knot to stay like this forever: beautiful like fragrant paper, impervious to the glazing eyes of dangerous men and the flickers of unknown shadows.

Strapped

I remember her eyes the color of pearl grey.

I volunteered for a suicide operation.

The girl confessed as we passed flowers like luxurious paper disappearing in faint sunlight. *But the men refused me.*

The girl trailed beside me as birds circled above black-greentrees, sailing the sky like paper butterflies.

Let's cross the dirt road, drain away sorrow in absolute silence and feel the heat of another summer in Srinagar.

I was humiliated. What else could I do?

The girl painted herself as the perfect bomber, wanting to be rewarded with Paradise for a life, unfulfilled and unloved.

Now, you, too, are a witness.

We walked through tumbleweeds and uneven rock as shopkeepers watched us enter an old building hit by bullets.

I am selfless, brave and resilient.

They say we are all capable of evil, small and big, and nothing haunted me more than ideology born of hate.

I am committed to change. Someone must listen.

She reached for my hand, and we continue walking under the chalky sunlight. We are strangers still.

I am single and strong. No one can stop me.

She imagined herself to be the next martyr and expected a Heavenly reward for giving up this life for the next.

I am not invisible. Even if you see us as ghosts.

The road came to an end. The girl believed the right time had come for her to begin a new movement.

We are want the same freedom. The only difference is that we are fighting, and you don't have to.

The girl surrendered to something greater than herself. In her   mind, she had nothing to lose.

85

With You

We watch the sky turn lavender, salmon and yellow.
You lean forward to smell my skin, and gift me
with words, unfamiliar, spoken in your language.
You hand me near-frozen yellow peonies,
and compare me to the flora of the valley,
always blooming in the background, spread across
the land in cropped form. *We are enough.*

On Love

The moon silvers the water, rising over banal rocks and inaccessible tracts of water and land.

We hold each other by the light of pearl and accept that we may never know each other's past.

We live in an uncertain present where maps dissolve like sugar to create new borders.

You say in a soft, sweet voice: *You don't need to know this place to love me.*

Blackboots

Exiled men whispered about dark, ghostly nights when the familiar sound of black boots stormed across the valley looking for suspects, half-asleep. The men searched for new land in dappled sun, trampling over bush and weed to start again.

They will never forget the golden light of the valley and all the colors that stretched across the hills. The exiles would like to forget men in black boots and fired weapons chasing them, running through hills like a virulent storm.

Alternate Names
for Missing Boys

1. Maniacs

2. Madmen

3. Militants

4. Mental

5. Devils

6. Terrorists

7. Imbeciles

8. Sociopaths

9. Psychos

10. Crackpots

11. Sickos

12. Deviants

13. Lunatics

14. Pervs

15. Outliers

16. Radicals

17. Extremists

18. Revolutionaries

19. Losers

20. Protestors

21. Rule breakers

22. Thrill-seekers

23. Rebels

24. Neurotics

25. Bakrichod

26. Gandu

27. Harami

...and so on

Operation Crossfire

There are a million reasons to call for war,
more ways to kill a man (or boy), unjustly,
without notice and without humanity.

There are different tactics used in conflict,
a thousand or so devices to shred a soul,
without concern for what happens next.

There are hollowed excuses and speeches,
a tapestry of words spoken out loud,
without ethics as they choose violence.

There are ancient leaders who break rules,
pronounce policies to control a people,
without compassion or understanding.

There are traditions to ignite hate,
more ways to shatter values of life,
without empathy for the living.

There are multiple roads to death,
many directions to launch operations,
without worrying about long-term impact.

There are uncivilized men and nations,
with manners and morals, stony hearted,
without principles, only pretentious action.

Freedom to Love

The taste of water on your skin numbs
me from who you really are in this place.
You are held captive by conflict,
unable to love, freely.

Will you ever leave Paradise?

I imagine myself with you for a lifetime,
listening to your voice, warm and generous.
There is little to say when you lose hope,
and love brings temporary solace.

Will you find a way back to love?

You are searching for something new
in a valley of vertigo and perpetual pain.
You must embrace love to be loved,
and step out of conflict to start again.

What is love in the time of conflict?

The world you live in is savage, cruel,
indifferent to kindness and mercy.
I wake up to freedom and a swollen heart,
praying you will be free to love fully.

What is free love?

Every year, we make plans to meet,
feel love again in a far-away place.
What you say will carry me for a lifetime,
and I imagine your love, free and wild.

Wings

We are impatient to wait out the cold
and wait for the silence of winter to pass.
Soon, new grass and heavy-billed birds will
return by spring, and we wonder what it
might feel like to fly with wings on air.

New Land

The innocent stumbled across jagged mountain as men
slaughtered tribes along a shared border.

The evil eye cast a spell.

Grandmother left behind apple orchards and childlike
wonder to start a new life.

Theirs is a complicated history.

Millions moved, entered a broken country divided
along ethnic and religious fault lines.

Prayers and rituals did not save everyone.

It isn't hard to imagine their hearts filled with isolation as
they walked slowly along the ridge where empty graves sat
stonily.

Migration was unjust.

The sun began to slant to its golden hour over
towns in empty, open spaces.

Welcome to new land.

Grandmother cried for a lost valley and memories
of wild sheep on frescoed hills.

It's time to disown the past.

It is Here

When I enter a land without a country, I see
widows with open arms and pained eyes,
their stories buried in water-filled cracks.
Their hearts carry horrors unparalleled
and sweep over them like black wind.

It is here, I cry.

When I leave a valley with many names,
I feel the weight of stones, hundreds dead
in unmarked graves, lying alone in cold
forest, their names revealed in
history books and icons.

It is here, I break.

Kashmir is more than conflict and carnage.
The valley inspires artists to recreate
hills sculpted by the wind as trees
bend to birdsong and falcons
soar in soft pink light.

It is here, I belong.

FARHANA QAZI

Imperfection

We make a promise along the windy road,
the light of the silver-white stars on trees
and leaves beneath our feet as the
moon comes up from its quiet corner.

We find comfort in the sleeves of the pheran,
a loose gown of wool to protect against ice
crystals and a thin veil of snow in November
that opens our hearts to different kinds of knowing.

We speak of togetherness in thigh-high shrubs,
where fat stems of flowers disappear
until spring, and all that is left is bitter cold
and leafless chinar trees by the road.

We promise to stay small, sweet,
always worthy of love and belonging,
despite the darkness of curfewed nights
and icicles on stone fields.

We accept the changes of each season:
a bright, mango sun that warms the line of
perpetual snow; the noise of spring water;
and the patterning of fall leaves.

We wait for the cold to pass, the rising
of a new-moon and kiss our hands for
faith and friendship—we agree to love
imperfection and celebrate life.

Weeping Hearts

people arrived from mountains of green
and land with flattened, cold grass to comfort
the shrills of the lonely mother, who stood
barefoot on small white blossoms that trembled
in the breeze, begging the saints for wildflowers
that once lined the fence of her near-broken home

they watched her fall from the bridge when the sky
turned from silver white; they ran to save her,
when she wished for death to join her only son,
who disappeared one day in the high blues
of winter, while she called his name,
hoping he might hear her

she demanded to feel something more than pain
under a star-gushing universe, and wanted more
than storm warnings and heavy memories
of those already gone; she needed to be
called by another name: a survivor
seemed generic, cliche, and swollen

in time, they village knew they could not save her
from hugging stone fields, and they could not
spare her from future tragedies; almost
everyone except the lonely mother accepted
hard truths; and some longed to rush east
to the depths of the hidden sun

there were many more broken mothers, anguished
by nightmares and nocturnal storms, their eyes
weakened by unfinished portraits, lives
shortened by war and weeping hearts;
as more women fall into grief,
Kashmir barely survives.

Waiting for You

In this half-wakeful state when memories of love seem unforgettable, I look for the sun sinking beneath the hills in the east, and blood-and-orange leaves of the great chinar tree burn in small fires outside your window, the smoke trailing a watery violet sky.

We can make this work.

You call my name as an avalanche of snow slides along the hills of Pahalgam, and I listen to your breath, overwhelmed by sluggish, winter dreams threading between your eyes. You wonder if fragments of song, lost melodies, and the sound of freedom will return.

You can start again.

You are unaware of ice pressing down from the North, and lightning crawling on the back of the mountain as thunder cracks like a fallen forest, lifting sheets of ice and forcing traveling water to flow further along the fields, as love birds rise from emerald lake.

I have a lifetime to love you.

The storm passes and a lace of white glows from the dusk as the mountain shifts, snow softening to pearl as bird wings skirt the air. I hardly notice time shifting, pushing and pulling, as fists of light swallow nights of rain and a pained heart overshadows everything.

We are strong together.

In the landscape of yellows, blue-gold moonlight, and a patchwork of snowflakes, the spontaneity of living is not an option. We seek comfort in graying cumulus, the flicker of shadow and a box of colors dotting the hills.

You only have one life to feel.

The shine of your omnivorous eyes bring warmth to bitter cold months; and you create abundant joy with dreams, light and dark, a kaleidoscope of promises under an August moon as stars shoot through the night until heavy rain and lightning strikes fields of rice.

I will wait for you.

Azadi

Slowly, they put down their signs and move in different directions, their faces like wounded instruments. They will be back, the men say of women clad in black with beaten eyes. On the dusty road, women begin to disperse, blocked by police in khaki uniforms, waving batons the size of baseball bats. For years, they marched, chanted and shouted slogans of freedom.

In summer, their voices float in thick air: What do we want? Azadi! What do we need? Azadi! They cry for freedom; the one with tired eyes leads the group, stepping over gravel, as the golden sun drifts behind clouds. On endless black nights, their words stretch between the stars and the shadow of time; they will not be forgotten by white noise and distant gunfire. They will march again when the curfew is lifted.

Stranger Things

I imagine the brightest sun in a valley fit for kings and mountains made of jewels; in its picture-perfect quality, locals search for ancient wisdom, poems by lovers, now lost to rulers who scorched the rights of people. This is the place fanned by leaves of gold and sap-green hills.

The valley is as fragile as its people. I hear tales of kings reclining on soft skin under shades of sun and a silver night sky. Mythical stories are whispered and soon to be forgotten by the new generation, exploring the foothills in a long afternoon's heat.

We imagine freedom as predawn light extinguishes the stars in winter and falcons cling to half-frozen branches. Here, we are forced to live with stranger things: the sound of boots at every corner; the silence of women muted by grief; and every mountain taken by the army.

Light and Shadow

In the solace of open spaces, we adapt to long winter months with silent strength, sighing at the chilled earth and the tapestry of grass and flowers buried deep in snow.

When the living green turns into cold scarlet, the air like ice on our faces, we listen to bitter rain, and pray that wisps of snow will be swallowed by the earth.

Yesterday, we walked to Zero Bridge overlooking the gray, still water and blue dusk, boats floating like small stones until the weight of a polar ice wind bellows at the lake.

In the color of silent white, we share multiple languages unfolding like indecipherable leaves on placid water, each word a memory of this marvelous place.

We turn to the earth's face adrift over lines of mountains and mounds of green. In every direction, Kashmir's light and shadow will last many lifetimes.

Paradise Lost

They remember a once glorious Kashmir ungoverned by armies of brown spanning mountains of flat-topped clouds with beaming eyes and heartbreaking control.

Locals dream of pale coral light at the break of dawn when they are free to smell the rain under a full moon. They love the smell of hills perfumed with windfall and sun; lovers rejoice in songs of old, their faces polished in pearl light.

The natural rhythms of the fields, acres of rice unharmed and saffron in October undamaged by war, thrive like displaced objects, settle into the earth and a robe full of bright light.

The original owners of Kashmir quietly sneer at men hiding behind chicken wire-wrapped towers and cinema houses converted into bunkers. They mock the murky occupiers.

The army threatens an ancient way of life and changes the social fabric of Kashmir. Along the valley's foothills are mighty heroes kept alive by memories of people, young and old.

Locals are unafraid of sirens in black streets and wait for the first sight of white puff clouds at dawn. Living under threat, they find comfort in brilliant light, the star and the moon, everything eternalized, fire and gravity.

Paradise is lost and found. Kashmir is Heaven enough.

FARHANA QAZI

Changing Light

From the guesthouse, I see falcons dusted with frost rest on
almost-bare branches, their eyes, amazingly clear and quiet.
We collect candles and water in ice-cold glasses.

There is no heat here!

The worker stays with me and reads a martyr's story as the
temperature continues to drop. Before dark, he brings a
bucket of hot water to my room.

Imagine living like this!

By night, the pipes are frozen and dangerously cold;
all around me, icicles form on rooftops and and roads
disappear into the black-darkness.

There is danger of dying cold!

In the morning, bands of warm light sculpt the valley long enough for big trucks to trudge along blunt slopes and slide by tall spruce trees covered in snow.

The army is on patrol!

The ice, miles thick, flows down hills as the sun pulls itself up, closing the space between cold wind and a painted white ground. As light fades, the worker returns to read again.

Someone will die tonight!

When I am alone, I watch the changing light, ice melting, water mixing with mounds of dirt as it slips out of the earth; hours later, I pray to the rising of a mosaic blue moon.

Nothing survives in cold!

Ephemeral

On the lower slopes of the mountain, a feathery pink sky extends across the landscape in abstract form as foreigners glide the Dal in shikaras, excited by the new horizon and the blending of colors that makes them want for more purity and transcendence, more blue and infinite white. They capture an ephemeral moment that will disappear only too fast, never to be repeated. If only it were possible to see the valley as more than beating hearts and the dead buried in unseen ground.

FARHANA QAZI

Under Siege

Despite the senseless violence,
and villages under siege, they lived
with purpose: driven by imagination
and undefined inspiration, they cherish
a landscape rounded by hillside cliffs,
gushing water, and bold evening stars.

Beauty outlives tragedy, they say aloud,
even as tanks pass them by; they turn to
the sky, pray in thunderous whispering
to calm quivering hearts and homes
crippled by decades-long grief.

In the orange screen of sunset, they walk,
one by one, to perform the evening
ritual, rising and falling to a leader who
offers infinite possibilities in a time of
distress and daily disorder.

The army arrives like thunder and leaves
behind a foul of charcoal smoke in the
world's most guarded place. Is there anything
left in the sound of the enemy's breath?
Is there anything more damning than a child
sleeping with eyes wide open?

Kashmir is under siege.

FARHANA QAZI

The Flood

A waspy wind opened the sepals of flowers and the long neck of the river poured over cities, towns and villages, beating against green summer grass as water snaked across cities like a serpent.

Piles of gravel and granite flowed to the surface; a torrential rain cursed animal and plant life, tumbling across centuries of stream beds and creeks. Is this hard rain?

Thunder wrested control of the valley, subverting its rage on silent harmony and more water sailed southward to infuriate the river, numbing the ground with waves of rain rumbling downward into the night.

A riverbank began to swell over the throat of soft, green hills and flattened tulip gardens, destroying nearly everything in the valley, except the moon ringed with its halo of light.

The deepening blue and black of night folded into daylight, revealing the fragility of the million-darted rain as it leashed unprecedented damage: bridges broken; hotels submerged; power lines undone; and dogs drifted in putrid water.

A foul smell saturated the air as the river opened to human waste in contaminated brown-red water, carcasses of cows on the surface floor; within days, timeless beauty transformed into a gray ocean of disease. It's unsafe to walk, they said.

Villages mourned the loss of sun-softened rice fields and orchards of apples; surviving walnut trees and warm-gold flowers wilted on the road like emblems of a dying sun.

Seasons of water, its swirling whites, blues and grays, with the power to impose death over a valley of petals, would become another a tragic memory, unfolding like paper flowers.

Spring

The whites and yellows of flowers in the castle of Mughals are strong and imposing, imbuing an innocence of tender times long gone, an epic era of danceand-song, of religious rituals coming undone.
The stories of kings with fairies for wives looking up at a night sky speckled with tiny silver stars open their hearts like fledgling birds, growing more sensual and sensitive to the sound of whispers.

In the daylight, as water lilies drift like ornaments in heaven along Nageen Lake, the ancient wake to spring's heraldic colors of primrose and indigo-blue and long for the serenity of nights. When heavy-billed birds return by spring, the valley rises, awakened like a child under moonlight, and again, everything is brilliant and bright.

For a moment, Kashmir feels new and safe.

To Feel Again

In the light, the valley turns gold and green. The young lover feels the timeless quality of his ancient land in splashes of ivy-green in distant hills, layers of clouds brushing against mountains, and splashes of gold in gardens by the lake.

It is here. In Paradise, he finds someone to love.

He scans the sky swirling along the edge of blues, this beautiful study of life. With a lightness of spirit, he holds her tightly, in the beat of a wing, smooth as the flight of kingfishers. He feels again, bursting into song, and in the act of singing, he is filled with love, healing, and the rhythm of her heart.

It is here. In Paradise, he let go of his demons.

Before he is called, the lover wants to feel one last time. He promises eternity as he holds her breath, speaks in metaphors, and asks for loyalty even as he leaves her to hide. *Because we are all dying in a valley of black holes, light nail-deep into ground unseen; we will meet after death.*

It is here. In Paradise, he runs towards the light.

Nothing Left to Say

In Kashmir, there is extraordinary love.
The suffering live with compassion,
holding onto secrets in private spaces
and shelter the tears of mothers.

There is nothing worse than fear.
In soft candlelight, women gather
to reveal their sorrows and untold truths
buried deep in their hearts.

In the valley, the inevitable madness
of time and mountains of green flattened
by violence and men in boots trampling
the earth strips away at normalcy.

There is nothing left to say when
numbed by pain and obscurity;
and women know that every tragedy
goes unnoticed, unrecorded.

The Beloved

In the city, there was manic energy, an intellectual freedom for cafe revolutionaries opposed to detention, deaths, and disappearances. By day, they talked. By night, they promised a future that no one has yet seen. The men with black or brown shiny hair, big luminous eyes, and welcoming smiles, knew how to stir hearts. They began each morning by thanking the Beloved, and offered expressions of hope, before stepping into rain, water flowing out of the soil, growing wider and deeper as the valley swells from another storm.

In the village, a rebel without a weapon picked a fight with words, argued with men in boots for his right to swim under the sound of the river, rushing, or a decision he made to walk into the sun, even on restricted national holidays, as the sun beamed gold on a tapestry of fallen leaves. He stood, unabashed, in front of black boots and argued without cursing, unprotected, when he knew too well the risk of speaking up; he could be shot or worse, wounded for acting independently.

Back in the city, an older woman, once jailed for a false terrorism charge, positioned herself as a rebel, alone and fearless. She held the microphone in the middle of the street, protestors by her side, and shouted to anyone listening. The valley belongs to us! She called for freedom for a people

intimidated, suppressed for decades, forced into a life of violence and fear, when all they deserved is peace. The Beloved is aware of the conflict.

But that was only the beginning. Encounters were planned; covert operations organized with careful precision; and a fearful and perceptive local population sensed the dangers ahead. The cafe rebels found new hiding places; outspoken women waited inside their homes for something to happen. In a place haunted by sorrow and secrecy, the facts of everyday life were soon forgotten, erased from news stories and mainstream media outlets. No one, except those living in the valley, could describe the wave of blood and hate unleashed on everyone.

As the valley erupted in ashes and flame, every living creature felt anger and anxiety; agitation and alarms sounded from every corner, and a new street uprising was born to provoke the men in black boots for erupting old fervor and intensifying violence. The old ways of manipulation could not erase memories of oppression, sagas of occupation and struggle, from a people's lived experience. The occupier's story and untruths died in the fighting and a new national self-identity was born.

From the cerulean blue sky, the Beloved watched the dead buried in the martyrs' graveyard, including children with

musical voices and light hearts; women prayed endlessly for
peace as the occupier brutally silenced unarmed civilians.
The vengeful pinned blame on an exaggerated militancy,
a band of missing boys who ran into black forests. As
more died, an ancient animosity reignited, blood and fire
aggravated by anything, on any day, that rustled in the air.

The Beloved, locals believed, lifted the hearts of the dying
and promised them that this life is nothing compared to
the next life, an eternal place of love and joy. The survivors'
guilt and pain passed over the earth's shadow, and they soon
learned to breathe again, looking for solace in shooting stars
and carrying little ones out of hiding and into a world of play.

Moon, Rising

The moon silvers the water, rising over banal
rocks and inaccessible tracts of water and land.

We hold each other and scan different horizons held by the
light of pearl; the blue glow of snow thickens our silence.

In quietude, we are like strangers, protected by the past and
live in an uncertain present and unplanned future.

The light flushes the boundaries between us, and we learn to
let go of carved spaces so we can walk again.

Memories of this place are enough to last lifetimes; we imagine
how hard it must be to search for something else.

In the moon, rising, we find solace in the Beloved; we look to
the sky to unburden longing hearts.

Someday, you will make me laugh again.

Nine Ways to Say Darkness

The Beloved said, *Let there be light!*
And light poured over the valley in waves,
a stream of brilliance revealed gold hues
and green-blue colors in abundance.

Until darkness weaved through the day,
obscuring bands of warm light; the sun
lost its splendor, its glorious flames of red,
shades of pink and purples reduced to black.

Then the elders taught children the truth,
of shadows, darker than night, that spilled
across the valley in layers, multitudes
of darkness staining all light. Forever.

We learned to read eyes in the dark,
looked for shadowy figures in somber
streetlight; searched for silhouettes in inky
sky, on nights when the moon never came.

The indistinct whispers at nightfall
did not respond to our fears; it was bred
in darkness, under starless skies, taht
we should admire the nebulous.

We forgot the glory of light, and soon
learned the nine ways to say darkness:
the ground swollen with horrors, unspoken /
murky / blackened / somber / inhumane /
hopelessness / nightmares, thick / the aphotic
depths of the heart, broken / injustice

The Beloved said, *Be patient and grateful!*
And hope streamed through the valley like
fast-moving water, eager to change and
brighten the the darkest of hearts.

Unthinkable

Locals whisper about dark, ghostly nights when the familiar sound of black boots stormed across the valley; the army searched for boys and men half-asleep with their shoes on, prepared and ready to be taken.

Boots stomp on sacred ground, across acres of land in dappled sun, trampling over a place where green, blue, and gold light shine over hills and brown-pleat cliffs. It is here that the innocent wait for the unthinkable to happen.

Closer to Love

It is easy to cling onto your warm eyes
and want more of what was once forbidden.

You sing an ancient song and make promises
to live forever with love and loyalty.

They have tried to criticize and isolate you
from feeling, but you find a way past judgement.

Inside of you, there is darkness and light,
flames and angels to bring you back to me.

Cold

We are not patient to wait out the cold, so we escape
to the north and wait for spirals of white frost to melt.

We often curse when we shouldn't.

And the snow is a paradox and the ice a riddle.

We pray this season passes so we can run in buttercup sun.

In our southern village, the snow steals sleep and joy.

After all these years, we still don't know how to live
without power and light.

We crawl inside each other's skin and speak in a multitudes of
verbs.

*Come closer, hold me tightly, make love, drink from my mouth,
fall in my arms, sleep quietly.*

Entangled in love, we forget trees emptied of fruit and
flowers lying under a parachute of blue-ice.

In the warm light, we dance with words.

With you by my side, I am uncaged, unafraid in the
dark-darkness where tragedies float.

I slide out of the black nest and move into eyes of
passion and flame.

Memories, 1940's

They traveled in uncomfortable silence with bare feet. Men with blades slaughtered tribes of people crossing borders made of imaginary lines; the innocent stumbled and died along dirt roads and jagged mountains. The dead, young and old, shout obscenity for the pain of Partition—a forced (unnecessary) exile imposed by bullies guised as colonials. Grandmother joined the exodus as a child, the events of 1940s alive in the folds of her memory.

We can't hold onto the past with a vengeance. I don't have the right to forgive the torturers: only God can do that.

Bones scattered among wild sheep and buried in frescoed hills; their souls may never reconcile with the great tragedy. Grandmother described an agitated relocation, a time of defeat and surrender of families, ethnicities, and entire identities folded into new nationalities: India and Pakistan.

No one had the power to crush the untouchables. They took everything. We lost farms, homes, and something more: our dignity.

Women, children, and men in sweat carried only the essentials as the crooked reclaimed land they didn't own. Millions moved across fault lines. Grandmother entered a new broken country, divided and threatened by leaders who died too soon. In migration, people were made to feel small and sapped of their honor to exist.

In time, we started over. There are only two choices: life or death. Choose life because you can.

Some stayed inside their ancestral homes, unprotected and open to attack. They refused to walk into the unknown: the daredevil of exile had no guarantee of life. Even in Kashmir, locals bled and the dead ascended to heaven, greeted by angels and messengers, or at least that's what the living said.

They are not dead. They are the faithful. They are not weak. They are strong and can finally rest in peace.

Mercy

Beautiful souls internalize everything,
count every blessing

They hold onto hearts no longer beating,
cultivating stories to keep them alive

Through each season, they chant
freedom and bury losses into the earth

Empathetic hearts absorb pain
with simple words and big gestures

They admire the star and moon,
and promise angels and messengers

Never once do they surrender honor
to the insensitive and selfish rulers

They pray for better days ahead and
know the Beloved is always present

Though time is not on their side,
they know togetherness is their strength

And their mercy is a love imbued
with gratitude in this short life

FARHANA QAZI

The Things We Said

We make vows on the windy road,
moving at the light of silver-white stars and
a sapphire moon rising from its quiet corner.

We wrap ourselves in the wool of the *pheran*
to protect against ice crystals and a thin veil
of snow in the darkest nights of January.

We speak of togetherness in thigh-high shrubs
of *Pari Mahal*, where fat stems of flowers disappear
until spring and all that is left is bitter cold.

We promise to stay small, sweet, forgiving,
always worthy of love and belonging
even when the valley is not ours to own.

We accept the changes of each season:
mango-colored sunlight over perpetual snow;
the sound of spring; and the pattering of leaves.

Faith

Women adorn other women
with words of comfort;
they greet one another
with open hearts

The Beloved is with us.

Women learn to conceal
collective tragedies
and rejoice in simple
beauties of life

The Beloved has a plan for us.

Women guard children in fields
flying kites under a cobalt sky,
aware of anyone, watching

The Beloved is in control.

Women carry memories of loved
ones bruised, battered, broken
through dollops of snow

The Beloved is not indifferent to us.

Women do not look for answers
from an inhumane oppressor
but turn to the sky for hope

The Beloved protects our hearts.

Thank You

Dear Reader,

If you appreciated this book, please leave a review on Amazon and other bookseller sites. Reviews are important and greatly valued.

If you want something new, please join the newsletter.

https://farhanaqazi.com/

A Call to Action

Over the years, so many people have asked me: what can I do to help? How can I support the Kashmiri people? The first step is awareness. Please share your knowledge of Kashmir to build understanding. Another vital step is empowering local women. I support local village women in Indian-held Kashmir to improve their lives. These women weave shawls from their homes and neighborhood co-ops to support their families. Your purchase of this book will help the women of Kashmir. Thank you for caring.

Stay in touch and join the newsletter for new work.

https://farhanaqazi.com/

Acknowledgments

I am profoundly grateful to the people of Kashmir who welcomed me into their private spaces so that I could see and feel the beauty of Kashmir.

I am indebted to my guides, who protected me as I wandered through the valley to experience the beauty of a war-torn valley. To my fans and life-long partner, who listened to these verses as I was writing them. Best of all, this book is for my late grandmother, and my spirited mama, who gifted me stories of Kashmir.

About the Author

FARHANA QAZI
Scholar. Speaker. Storyteller

Farhana Qazi is an award-winning speaker and scholar on conflicts in the Muslim world. Born in northern Pakistan and raised in Texas, she straddles the East and West and brings multiple perspectives to her work.

Farhana is the first American-Muslim woman to serve in the Counter-Terrorism Center in the U.S. government. As a young analyst, she studied conflicts and briefed senior policy makers and practitioners. For her service, she received Presidential recognition and multiple awards from the the U.S. government and military for teaching them how to build relationships with people on the ground.

Farhana has taught classes on global conflict at The George Washington University. She is a recipient of the 21st Century Leader Award, presented by the National Committee on American Foreign Policy in New York, for her training and service to the U.S. military, and she received the Distinguished Humanitarian Award from her alma mater for her reporting on women in war.

As an expert, Farhana has appeared in mainstream media: CNN, the BBC, PBS, National Public Radio, Fox News, CSpan, Bloomberg, ABC News, MSNBC, Canadian national television, Voice of America, Al Jazeera, and more. She is a graduate of the National Security Studies Program at the George Washington University and holds a Bachelor of Arts with a major in Political Science and a minor in French from Southwestern University in Georgetown, Texas.

Farhana lives in many places. She loves the outdoors and powerful books that change lives. To learn more about her writing, visit www.farhanaqazi.com

www.ingramcontent.com/pod-product-compliance
Lightning Source LLC
LaVergne TN
LVHW011158080426
835508LV00007B/471